How To Know God Better & Love Yourself More

Living a Vocal, Valued and Victorious Life (Vol. 3)

JO ANNE MEEKINS

Inspired 4 U

Publications

Published by Inspired 4 U Publications,
an imprint of Inspired 4 U Ministries, LLC.

September 2014

ISBN-13: 978-0692289419
ISBN-10: 0692289410

DEDICATION

I dedicate this book to everyone who has ever desired to know God better and love themselves more, but have struggled through the process and have felt like for every two steps forward, they took three steps back.

Be encouraged, knowing that it is a journey of a lifetime with many levels of learning. And remember, God knows the details and has already worked everything together for your good.

I share these tips, tools and techniques with you to learn and implement for your own healing, growth and transformation.

Be blessed, One LOVE!

Jo Anne Meekins
Inspired 4 U

CONTENTS

*"Behold, I have indelibly imprinted (tattooed a picture of) you
on the palm of each of My hands; [O Zion]
your walls are continually before Me."*
(Isaiah 49:16)

ACKNOWLEDGMENTS

With a full heart of gratitude and love, I acknowledge God, the Father, Son, and Holy Spirit for their grace, strength and guidance in the completion of this book and thus, the completion of the Living a Vocal, Valued and Victorious Life 3-volume series.

I Thank You, my Triune God, for restoration, elevation, favor and an enlarged territory. I appreciate Your patience with me learning my lessons, in my spiritual development, and my transformation.

Because You never gave up on me; preplanned my victory; taught me how to heal, persevere and rise; and how to BE LOVE and receive love, I am one grateful somebody, who is in love with YOU!

HOW GOD CREATED THE WORLD AND EMPOWERS YOU TO CREATE YOURS

World Creation

I believe that the world was created by the spoken Word. God created the world and all it contains by progressively speaking and shaping it into existence in six days. Genesis, the first book of the bible, describes how the earth started out as formless, empty, dark, and watery before God said "Let there be light," calling the light Day and the darkness Night on the first day. On the second day, God spoke and made a firmament (an expanse; a wide space) to divide the waters; He called the firmament above the waters Heaven. On the third day, God gathered the waters beneath the firmament into seas and the appearing dry land He called Earth. At His word, the earth brought forth grass, seed yielding herbs, and fruit trees. On day four, God made the sun, moon and stars in the heavens to give light on the earth and to divide the light from the darkness.

Sea creatures and winged birds were created on the fifth day to fill the waters and multiply on the earth respectively. On the sixth day, God brought forth cattle, every creeping thing, and beasts of the earth, each according to its kind; and then He created male and female to be fruitful and multiply, fill and subdue the earth, and have dominion over every living thing that swims in the seas, and moves on and flies over the earth.

This is how I think the world was created as read, taught, and believed from the Holy Bible. I also believe that just as God spoke the World into existence, He has given us the power and authority to speak into our own lives and the lives of others to co-create the social and private worlds we live in.

Human Creation

We are spiritual beings living a human experience, created in God's image with dominion over all other created works, and taught to call those things that do not exist as though they did. I believe that if you don't like what you see, change what you say!

When I was a child, there was a saying that "Sticks and stones may break my bones, but names will never harm me." It wasn't true then and it's not true now. Words do HURT! There is power in words and words in the form of rumors, slander, vengeance, and jealousy have been known to emotionally and physically (in some situations) scar, wound, and destroy individuals, families, and communities. Think of the children who are constantly put down, being told that they are no good and will never amount to anything. Some rise to the challenge and prove their critics wrong, but far too many live down to the negative low expectations spoken into their lives.

The bible describes the tongue as a fire, a world of evil among the parts of the body, corrupting the whole person … a restless evil full of deadly poison (James 3: 6, 8). We have the ability to speak blessings or curses into our lives and the lives of others. Which type does your world reflect? Has your life and surroundings taken on the beauty and fruitfulness of God's spoken creation or does your soul feel dry and your neighboring gardens appear to be dying?

Words can also HEAL! Implement the following steps to progressively shape your world:

1. Begin to speak positive affirmations and faith confessions to yourself daily and build up the people in your life.

2. Learn to say what you mean and mean what you say, in love. Be careful of your attitude, tone, and volume when you speak.

3. See yourself and others through the spiritual eyes of God and know that we are all fearfully and wonderfully made with a plan and a purpose to prosper, and have hope, and a future.

4. Align yourself with God's will for your life, be obedient to His direction, speak what you desire to experience personally and professionally; and then expect God to do a new thing, exceedingly abundantly more than you can think or ask.

The power of life and death is in the tongue, choose to speak LIFE!

REFLECTIONS OF THE REDEMPTIVE RECONCILING RESURRECTION

As a child, Easter represented decorated goodie baskets, colored eggs, chocolate bunnies, jelly beans, dress-up in pretty frilly dresses with crinoline slips underneath, and some of my favorite foods for dinner. But when I became older and gained a knowledge of and personal relationship with God, I learned and appreciated the significance of Christ's Calvary Crucifixion and the power of the Redemptive Reconciling Resurrection!

"When I was a child, I spoke as a child, I understood as a child, I thought as a child; but when I became a man, I put away childish things." (1 Corinthians 13:11)

As an adult, Easter represents the Resurrection of Christ and the ultimate sacrifice that led up to it. As I revisit the biblical meaning of Easter, be open to the resurrection of your spirit with the nurturing restorative power of God's word and His immeasurable unconditional LOVE.

DEFINING EVENTS

Lent: A period of penitence and fasting observed on the 40 weekdays from Ash Wednesday to Easter by many churches. — Webster's Dictionary

Easter: A feast that commemorates Christ's resurrection. — Webster's Dictionary;

(English) Passover events. (Greek) pascha (paś-khah) the Passover (the meal, the day, the festival or the special sacrifices connected with it). — Strong's Dictionary

Passover: a Jewish holiday celebrated in March or April in commemoration of the liberation of the Hebrews from slavery in Egypt [from the exemption of the Israelites from the slaughter of the firstborn of Egypt (Exodus 12:23-27)]. — Webster's Dictionary;

(Hebrew) Pâcach (paw-sakh) to hop, i.e. (fig.) skip over (or spare); Pecach (peh'-sakh) a pretermission, i.e. exemption; used only technically of the Jewish Passover (the festival of the victim): - Passover (offering). — Strong's Dictionary

Resurrection: the rising of Christ from the dead; the rising again of all the human dead before the final judgment; Resurgence, revival. — Webster's Dictionary;

(English) rising from death. (Greek) anastasis (an-as'-tas-is) a standing up again, i.e. (lit.) a resurrection from death (individual, genitive case or by implication), or (fig.) a (moral) recovery (of spiritual truth): — raised to life again; Ĕgĕrsis (eg'-er-sis) a resurgence (from death); Ĕgĕirō (eg-i'-ro) to waken (tran. or intr.), i.e. rouse (lit. from sleep, from sitting or lying, from disease, from death; or fig. from obscurity, inactivity, ruins, nonexistence): - awake, lift (up), raise (again, up), rear up, (a-) rise (again, up), stand, take up. — Strong's Dictionary

THE SACRIFICE

"For God so loved the world that He gave His only begotten Son, that whoever believes in Him should not perish but have everlasting life."
(John 3:16)

Many people question God when they lose a loved one, as if God is cruel, indifferent, and can't identify with the pain of grief. Yet, God put a plan in place from the beginning of time to sacrifice His only Son as payment, an offering for our sins, that we could reestablish a right relationship with God the Father. Jesus Christ was born to live an unblemished, humble, selfless life; die as our redemption fee; and be resurrected in all power, removing the stain of sin and the sting of death.

Although salvation is free to us, the provisions for receiving it were costly to God, who understood all too well the magnitude of freeing mankind from the bondage of sin. God saw and also experienced the pain that can be associated with love, as Jesus all knowingly and willingly endured attempts on His life, betrayal from a close friend, mockery, scorn, spit, unspeakable torture, humiliation, and being nailed to a cross for you and me.

There are some of us who may dare to die for a loved one, like a child or a spouse. However, I don't think anyone would be able to handle the fore-knowledge of how and when that opportunity might present itself or if knowing the violent and excruciatingly painful details in advance, not attempt to conveniently change the experience or wimp out in the end. But, Jesus did it for those He loved and for those who are challenging to love.

"For while we were still without strength, in due time Christ died for the ungodly. For scarcely for a righteous man will one die; yet perhaps for a good man someone would even dare to die. But God demonstrates His own love toward us, in that while we were still sinners, Christ died for

us. Much more then, having now been justified by His blood, we shall be saved from wrath through Him." (Romans 5:6-9)

God is acquainted with the pain of separation and death. As a man, Jesus bore our sorrows and carried our grief; He was wounded for our transgressions and bruised for our iniquities. As the ultimate sacrificial lamb, Jesus (our Passover) died that we might be free.

"In fact, the law requires that nearly everything be cleansed with blood, and without the shedding of blood there is no forgiveness."
(Hebrews 9:22)

THE RESURRECTION

Praise God the story didn't end at the Cross! After the crucifixion, Jesus' body was laid in a borrowed tomb and when some of the women followers had come to the tomb, He had risen as He said. *"And God both raised up the Lord and will also raise us up by His power"* (1 Corinthians 6:14). The resurrection of Christ fulfills the prophecy and the promise of overcoming death in Adam by being made alive in Christ. For those of us who confess with our mouth the Lord Jesus and believe in our hearts that God raised Him from the dead, we are saved from sin and death, and can experience life anew in Christ on earth and eternally in heaven.

We do not have to wait until our bodies expire and Jesus returns to experience a resurrection. We can live a resurrected life right here and now by knowing Him better and the power of His resurrection. The Holy Spirit, who was at work in Him, is a seal deposited in us guaranteeing our inheritance and will teach us all things and renew us daily. Jesus came that we might have an abundant life by following His example of obedience, humility, and service to others unto God.

Living a Spirit-filled life will empower us to overcome

sinful habits, forgive the unforgivable, love unconditionally, persevere through pain, and face our fears, which will open the door for God to work all things together for our good, and do exceedingly abundantly above all that we ask or think.

'Jesus said to her, "I am the resurrection and the life. He who believes in Me, though he may die, he shall live." (John 11:26)

A RESURRECTION EXPERIENCE

You can experience the resurrection,
God deemed it so before time had begun,
for God so loved the world
that He gave His only begotten Son.

You can experience the resurrection
when you open your heart to Jesus Christ;
You can go through and overcome
the stress, the struggles, and the strife.

You can experience the resurrection
when your past discretions no longer hurt,
and you don't care if the truth comes out
when so called friends try to dish old dirt.

You can experience the resurrection
when you have joy instead of pain,
when you praise God in the midst of battle
before the victory has been obtained.

You can experience the resurrection,
growing in the power of Jesus Christ.
You can experience the resurrection
Because He got up after laying down His life!

"That I may know him, and the power of his resurrection, and the fellowship of his sufferings, being made conformable unto his death."
(Philippians 3:10)

VITAL ELEMENTS IN DEVELOPING AN INTIMATE RELATIONSHIP WITH GOD

Intimacy is established when you grow beyond just knowing about someone to the experience of personal knowledge from spending quality time in their presence. In order to develop an intimate relationship with God, it is necessary to cultivate your relationship using the following spiritual elements:

FAITH: You must first believe in God and what is written in His word. It is impossible to please God without faith; and in order to have faith, you must first hear the good news about Christ. Therefore, you must both read the Word for yourself and make yourself available to hear the Word, whether it be in church, online, a podcast, or the telephone.

HOLY SPIRIT: The Holy Spirit deals with the inner man and connects you to God and others by faith through Jesus Christ. He also:

- Seals– Marks you to indicate ownership and promise;

- Guides– Directs you in the ways of God about what

He has heard from God the Father as it pertains to you;

- Intercedes– Prays on your behalf and others, in accordance to God's will.

TRANSFORMATION: Surrender your will, present your life to God and renew your mind. Be Christ-Minded in your thoughts and actions.

"And so, dear brothers and sister I plead with you to give your bodies to God because of all he has done for you. Let them be a living and holy sacrifice— the kind he will find acceptable. This is truly the way to worship him. ²Don't copy the behavior and customs of this world, but let God transform you into a new person by changing the way you think. Then you will learn to know God's will for you, which is good and pleasing and perfect." (Romans 12:1-2)

LOVE: God is love. If God is in you, then you are love also and will reflect this love to others.

"Dear friends, let us continue to love one another, for love comes from God. Anyone who loves is a child of God and knows God. ⁸But anyone who does not love does not know God, for God is love. ⁹God showed how much he loved us by sending his one and only Son into the world so that we might have eternal life through him." (1 John 4:7-9)

Experiencing true intimacy with God beyond a surface knowledge of Him is contingent upon your level of faith, the indwelling presence of the Holy Spirit, your willingness to transform, and your obedience to walk in love.

DISCERNING THE MAGNITUDE
OF GOD'S LOVE

To discern means to come to know, recognize, or discriminate mentally. Love is an action word, demonstrated in tangible ways. Think about the ways you show love to others, like family, friends, and romantic love interests. Also, reflect on how you desire love to be shown to you. Consider the ways that you know and experience love in the natural, as you read about the magnitude of God's love for you.

An inside view of God's Love for you

God's love is personal, empowering, longsuffering and merciful. He made us in His image with complete authority over the earth, a redemption policy, and a bottomless reservoir of compassion. God's love is everlasting, never failing, and inseparable from us.

Now consider for a moment God's ultimate sacrifice. God gave His only begotten Son because of His love for us. So not only did He choose to deal with the pain of that momentary loss, but also the excruciating method of the sacrifice. Can you think of anyone that you might dare to die for? Close your eyes, take a deep breath in, hold, exhale and reflect a minute ... Now, does anyone come to mind?

Some people adamantly believe that they would die for a loved one or risk their life to save an innocent, but add in the knowledge of how that death would come. Would they or you still do so if it would involve extreme physical torture and pain?

Well, Jesus not only died for the best and the worst of us, He did so knowing the horror of how death would come and allowed it anyway. Although, it was not without a momentary lack of willingness, as indicated in the following scripture:

"Father, if you are willing, take this cup from me; yet not my will, but yours be done." [43]An angel from heaven appeared to him and strengthened him. [44]And being in anguish, he prayed more earnestly, and his sweat was like drops of blood falling to the ground."
(Luke 22:42-44)

The "The Passion of Christ" movie gave a visually graphic portrayal of what Christ endured prior to and during the crucifixion. For me, it gave me a new appreciation for the song that says "the blood that Jesus shed for me way back on Calvary," and a new perspective on the magnitude of His love and commitment to redeem and reconcile mankind to the Father.

The magnitude of God's love is immeasurable and surpasses human understanding. He is love and in order for you to know and experience true, unconditional, agape love, you must enter into a personal relationship with Him through Jesus Christ.

Measure your love relationships against the standard of love demonstrated in God's word, and then become the love you seek and discern in God.

PRAYER POSTURES AND COMMUNICATION WITH GOD

Description

According to the New Bible Dictionary, prayer is worship that includes all the attitudes of the human spirit in its approach to God: Adoration, Confession, Praise, and Supplication. For me, it is a privilege that God makes available for us to commune together verbally, emotionally, mentally and physically to express praise, concerns, requests, thanksgiving, and adoration. It is to boldly come imperfect as I am, in an honest, open, and humble manner; in good times and perceived bad times, regardless of how I feel or my present circumstances, trusting that God's unconditional love and promises will prevail. Below, I examine some elements of prayer as experienced in my prayer life.

Intercessory Prayer:

- To lift up another person or situation in prayer;
- To go to God on behalf of someone else in order to help them through their life situations;
- To take on another's life issues and keep them before God as they fight through spiritual warfare;

- To allow the Holy Spirit to work through you to pray about specific needs in any and every area.

Ways I Pray

In my prayer sessions, I sometimes pray for myself, intercede on behalf of others, or join with one or more people. I enjoy my personal quiet time, but have also participated on prayer conference calls. And then, there are times when I call or text friends for needed prayer support. Matthew 18: 19 – 20 affirms the added power of group prayer in stating, "*Again, I tell you that if two of you on earth agree about anything you ask for, it will be done for you by my Father in heaven. For where two or three come together in my name, there I am with them.*"

When I pray, I do so using the word of God because I believe the promise in Isaiah 55:11 that states, "*It will not return to me empty, but will accomplish what I desire and achieve the purpose for which I sent it.*" God is accountable to His word.

I have also found that singing enhances my prayer life; when a song comes to mind, it seems to magnify God's presence in and around me ushering me into a more intimate experience.

Whether in word or thought, I pray while I am working, walking, talking, dancing, sitting, standing, kneeling, or lying prostrate.

Positive Prayer Factors

I have the confidence in His promises that:

1. Anything I ask according to His will, He hears and gives (1 John 5: 14-15).

2. I will have transcending peace to guard my heart and mind in Jesus (Philippians 4:6-7).

3. If I commit to the Lord whatever I do, my plans will succeed (Proverbs 16:3).

Another positive factor is the mutual exchange when I communicate with God. I receive direction and instructions for my life and He gives me the words to speak and write for others and myself (Isaiah 50:4). However, I think that the greatest benefit is the help in times of need and the intercession of the Holy Spirit when I don't know what to say or feel too stressed to pray (Romans 8:26-27).

Negative Prayer Factors

On the other hand, there are some factors that don't feel as pleasing or positive, such as the watching and waiting period; the unexpected answer; and the disappointing desired answer as described below:

- Sometimes waiting for God's deliverance, direction, or plan to unfold in my life creates anxiety, especially when His manifestation time is considerably longer than anticipated.

- Then there are times when the unexpected answer is a painful NO or comes by way of an injury, as in when my 15 year old niece died, no matter how passionately I pleaded; or when I received a financial blessing by way of a long term disabling accident.

- The old saying "Be careful what you pray for" comes to mind regarding the desired answer when you get what you prayed for only to find out that it was not what you thought and now no longer want.

Confident Prayer

Prayer is essential in order for God's people to effectively experience victorious living. To develop confidence in your prayer life, you need to know, believe, and speak God's word over your life and watch Him work the details out on your behalf. God's word is rich with promises that can encourage you to stand or hold on when going through challenging life experiences and rich with promises that can pump up your praise while you expectantly wait with excitement on what you know and believe to be true.

Read, meditate on, and seal the following scriptures in your heart to guide you to and through a confident prayer life filled with peace, joy, love, forgiveness and gratitude.

A Prayer Model

[5] *"And when you come before God, don't turn that into a theatrical production either. All these people making a regular show out of their prayers, hoping for stardom! Do you think God sits in a box seat?*

[6] *"Here's what I want you to do: Find a quiet, secluded place so you won't be tempted to role-play before God. Just be there as simply and honestly as you can manage. The focus will shift from you to God, and you will begin to sense his grace.*

[7-13] *"The world is full of so-called prayer warriors who are prayer-ignorant. They're full of formulas and programs and advice, peddling techniques for getting what you want from God. Don't fall for that nonsense. This is your Father you are dealing with, and he knows better than you what you need. With a God like this loving you, you can pray very simply. Like this:*

Our Father in heaven,
Reveal who you are.
Set the world right;

Do what's best—
as above, so below.
Keep us alive with three square meals.
Keep us forgiven with you and forgiving others.
Keep us safe from ourselves and the Devil.
You're in charge!
You can do anything you want!
You're ablaze in beauty!
Yes. Yes. Yes.

¹⁴⁻¹⁵ *"In prayer there is a connection between what God does and what you do. You can't get forgiveness from God, for instance, without also forgiving others. If you refuse to do your part, you cut yourself off from God's part.* (Matthew 6:5-15)

WAIT on God's Goodness:

"I remain confident of this:
I will see the goodness of the Lord
in the land of the living.
¹⁴ Wait for the Lord;
be strong and take heart
and wait for the Lord."
(Psalm 27:13-14)

How about you? What is your prayer life like? If you struggle in this area, I suggest you not focus on what to say or how long to say it. Just talk to God from your heart whenever you need and wherever you are, as often as possible. And you don't have to wait till something is wrong. God loves us to spend time with Him, we were created to worship Him and He is forever present. So give thanks too. There is always something to talk to God about and He is worthy of all praise.

Remember, prayer is simply a heart to heart conversation between you and God without form or fashion. Be yourself, come as you are, believe on His word and speak it back to Him in confidence. And when you don't know what to say, the Spirit himself will intercede for you with wordless groans. So pray confidently, trust God and WAIT expectantly and patiently for God to work in your favor. He will perfect the things concerning you (Psalm 138:8).

HOW TO OBTAIN MAXIMUM RESULTS
FROM GOD'S WORD

You can shift your consciousness and be empowered to move forward in the life that God has planned and purposed for you when you show up (regardless of how you feel and what is going on) to the places where your spiritual enlightenment, healing, growth and transformation are attainable. While a member of my former church and as someone who experienced the challenges of transition, new levels, and past issues, I showed up at Greater Faith Temple for prayer service and the Life Change Institute. There, I shifted into a renewed empowered attitude as I was reminded of who and whose I AM, and of the tools made available through prayer and God's word. Pastor Michel White-Haynes showed up in spite of the challenges in her life and taught us through physical demonstration and exhortation the following message and steps to obtaining maximum results from the word of God.

1. **STUDY**: We have to study the word in order to know God and understand it, remember it and live it.

"Study to show thyself approved unto God, a workman that need not be ashamed, rightly dividing the word of truth." (2 Timothy 2:15)

2. **HEAR**: What you repeatedly hear becomes a doctrine for your life. Channel what you hear.

"How can they hear without someone preaching to them? ...
¹⁷Consequently, faith comes from hearing the message, and the message is
heard through the word of Christ .... ¹⁵He who has ears, let him hear."
(Romans 10:14c, 17; Matthew 11:15)

3. **MEDITATE**: Ponder God's word, eat it, chew on it, and let it resonate.

"Blessed is the man ... his delight is in the law of the LORD,
and on his law he meditates day and night." (Psalm 1:1a, 2)

4. **KEEP**: Keep the word in your heart and forgive. Clean and protect your heart.

"Create in me a clean heart, O God, and renew a steadfast spirit
within me .... ²³Keep your heart with all diligence, for out of
it spring the issues of life." (Psalm 51:10; Proverbs 4:23)

5. **CONFESS**: Speak the word. Declare and decree the word of God over your circumstances. Make it come out of your mouth. Change your language because your words come to life.

"So tell them, 'As surely as I live,' declares the LORD, 'I will
do to you the very things I heard you say." (Numbers 14:28)

Be in agreement with what God's word says about your situations be it:

- Finances– My God shall supply all your needs (Philippians 4:19);

- Health– And by His wounds we are healed (Isaiah 53:5);

- Battles– No weapon formed against you will prevail (Isaiah 54:17); If God be for us, who can be against us?

HOW TO KNOW GOD BETTER & LOVE GOD MORE

We are more than conquerors (Romans 8:31, 37); Do not be afraid of them; the LORD your God himself will fight for you (Deuteronomy 3:22).

Trust God's word. What He says must be done. God's word will not return empty-handed, it will do the work He sent it to do and complete the assignment He gave it (Isaiah 55:11).

6. **PRAY**: Use God's word as your prayer language. Find the appropriate scripture that speaks to your need and pray it over that situation. Remind God of His promises over your life.

"The effective, fervent prayer of a righteous man avails much."
(James 5:16b)

7. **ACT**: You must put the word of God into action for it to work for you. Pay your tithes and see if He does not pour you out a blessing you don't have room enough to receive.

"¹⁰Bring the whole tithe into the storehouse, that there may be food in my house. Test me in this," says the LORD Almighty, "and see if I will not throw open the floodgates of heaven and pour out so much blessing that you will not have room enough for it."
(Malachi 3:10)

Serve God intentionally and with gladness. Hold your head up, smile and press through your challenges. Look better than what you may be going through. God is good all the time and worthy of our praises.

8. **OBEY**: Obedience to the word of God is the key to your blessing. To obey is to adhere and carefully carry out what the Lord requests, requires, and expects. You can no longer sit on the fence.

"Listen obediently, Israel. Do what you're told so that you'll have a good

life, a life of abundance and bounty, just as God promised, in a land abounding in milk and honey. (Deuteronomy 6:3)

"To obey is better than sacrifice." (I Samuel 15:22b)

The word of God is full of power and God's grace to change our lives. The Lord uses simple terms and familiar things to acquaint us with His word, such as lamp (unto our feet) and seed (sowing).

God is not wordy and will speak on our level so that we get the understanding to do what the word says. If the King James Version (KJV) is challenging to understand, read a different bible translation, such as the New Living Translation (NLT), The Message Bible (MSG), New International Version (NIV) or the Amplified Bible (AMP). Then, do the steps necessary to obtain maximum results from God's word.

HOW TO OPERATE WITHIN YOUR GOD-ENLARGED TERRITORY

The Territory

There is a harvest of souls lost in darkness within your sphere of influence and you are the light and love empowered to be a blessing. In 1 Chronicles 4:9, Jabez prayed for God to enlarge his territory and God granted his request. However, I surmise to you that you don't have to make that request because God has already enlarged your territory miles beyond the boundaries of your immediate family, friends, and workplace; and He has provided instructions for how you are to operate within your territory.

How do you respond to what you see?

What is your language and posture towards people in pain, lost, lonely, or temperamental, secretly seeking and thirsting to belong and believe in something or someone greater than themselves? For instance, what do you think and do when you encounter the following:

- A parent screaming or cursing at their child in public;

- School age children talking loud and acting out on public transportation or in the streets;

- A seemingly inattentive mother walking several feet ahead of her little child;

- People arguing and calling each other out of their name.

BE Christ-Like

God is no respecter of persons, He loves us all unconditionally and opens His arms to whosoever will receive Him. Therefore, it would behoove you to consider *What Would Jesus Do* (WWJD) and treat people accordingly, for the promise is extended to all He will call. With that in mind, I offer the following seven actions on how to operate within your God-enlarged territory:

1. **Be alert**: Observe your surroundings, the people, places, and things. You already possess the land and it is kingdom building time– time to intentionally grow the family of God by being Christ-Like.

2. **Be responsive**: Respond in love through language, posture, and attitude as the Holy Spirit leads. Remember the Good Samaritan in Luke 10:25–37. Love your neighbor as yourself; consider everyone as your neighbor, brother, or sister and show mercy. We are all ONE and there is only one appropriate response– God's LOVE!

3. **Be the love**: Project and amplify its power to erase all errors and break down all barriers until it is victorious as in St. Germaine's "I am the light of the heart" prayer. Practice this prayer or something similar and vibrate its message wherever you are when you feel or hear discord. Your territory has been enlarged by divine design. There are

desolate people in the land who need you to see them and respond in love.

I AM the Light of the Heart

Shining in the darkness of being

And changing all into the golden treasury

Of the Mind of Christ.

I AM projecting my Love out into the world

To erase all errors

And to break down all barriers.

I AM the power of Infinite Love,

Amplifying itself

Until it is victorious, world without end!

– St. Germain

4. **Respond with prayer**: It's okay if you don't know what to pray. Turn within and be open to Spirit, who will intercede on your behalf and others, as described in Romans 8:22-28.

5. **Pray on a broader scale**: When praying for personal issues, expand the prayer to include anyone and everyone who may be experiencing similar circumstances. Going through the pain of challenges makes you a prime heartfelt intercessor for others in that same situation. Pray for opportunities to be used by God.

6. **Judge not**: Don't react in judgment, leave the judgments to God and work out your own soul salvation.

Matthew 7:1-2 says, "*Do not judge, or you too will be judged. For in the same way you judge others, you will be judged, and with the measure you use, it will be measured to you.*"

7. **Continue your forgiveness work**: Practice the Ho'oponopono principle from Joe Vitale's book, "Zero

Limits," to help counter and release negative thoughts and emotions:

- As often as necessary, regarding anyone you need to forgive, privately and continuously repeat the phrase "I love you, I'm sorry, please forgive me, thank you."

Let go and let God, one moment at a time.

The work we do within extends without in transformative ways throughout our territories. Radiate high vibrations of love, forgiveness, and gratitude; and then watch God work a new thing in your own life and beyond.

HOW TO DEVELOP A BIBLICALLY-BASED ABUNDANCE MINDSET

Elements Defined

Many people equate wealth, abundance, and prosperity with having lots of money. However, while finances can be a manifestation of those things, it is not the all in all. Webster defines these elements of consciousness as:

Wealth: "Abundance of possessions or resources." Although finances are certainly considered as possessions and resources by those who have, finances are not specifically mentioned in the definition. Abundant possessions can also be family, friends, love, peace, and joy in addition to material items. It's a matter of perspective, how you perceive your situation. Abundant resources can include online information and the expertise, knowledge, and support available within such communities as prayer lines, coaching, and churches.

Abundance: "An ample or overflowing quantity" of those possessions and resources that are identified as wealth.

Prosperity: "The condition of being successful or

thriving." That conditioning must begin in the mind before it can translate into a physical manifestation, especially if it is to be maintained. There are many stories of people who have gotten rich suddenly, but ended up broker than when they started because they had not conditioned themselves to manage effectively what they acquired.

Points To Ponder

The following three points are offered to assist in developing and maintaining a mindset of wealth, abundance, and prosperity.

1. Present yourself in excellence and service to others, using what you have and are passionate about. Identify and develop your passion in a way that adds value to others and offer it for a money-energy exchange.

Proverbs 8:16 tells us that *"A gift [fee or present] opens the way for the giver and ushers him into the presence of the great."* Know that you are the gift and already have everything you need.

"Now to him who is able to do immeasurably more than all we ask or imagine, according to his power that is at work within us."
(Ephesians 3:20)

2. Shift your mind off money and focus on faith in what God says and is calling you to do. He will show you the way and make provisions when you seek Him first. Begin to count your blessings and be grateful for what you have instead of thinking in terms of lack. When I shared about my decision to resign from my corporate writing job to pursue ministry fulltime, some people responded with, "How are you going to live?" and "Will you be able to eat?"

I chose to step out in faith and focus on scriptures like Matthew 6:25-34, *"Therefore I tell you, do not worry about your life, what you will eat or drink; or about your body, what you will wear. Is not life more important than food, and the body more important than clothes? ²⁶Look at the birds of the air; they do not sow or reap or store away in barns, and yet your heavenly Father feeds them. Are you not much more valuable than they? ²⁷Who of you by worrying can add a single hour to his life? ²⁸"And why do you worry about clothes? See how the lilies of the field grow. They do not labor or spin. ²⁹Yet I tell you that not even Solomon in all his splendor was dressed like one of these. ³⁰If that is how God clothes the grass of the field, which is here today and tomorrow is thrown into the fire, will he not much more clothe you, O you of little faith? ³¹So do not worry, saying, 'What shall we eat?' or 'What shall we drink?' or 'What shall we wear?' ³²For the pagans run after all these things, and your heavenly Father knows that you need them. ³³But seek first his kingdom and his righteousness, and all these things will be given to you as well. ³⁴Therefore do not worry about tomorrow, for tomorrow will worry about itself. Each day has enough trouble of its own."*

"And my God will meet all your needs according to his glorious riches in Christ Jesus." (Philippians 4:19)

"Trust in the LORD with all your heart and lean not on your own understanding; ⁶in all your ways acknowledge him, and he will make your paths straight." (Proverbs 3:5-6)

3. Study your Holy Word or Sacred text. Get quiet and still before God, listen for instruction, and be obedient to what you hear. Take action, put feet under your dreams and walk it out. T.D. Jakes says, "It will work if you work it."

"Do not let this Book of the Law depart from your mouth; meditate on it day and night, so that you may be careful to do everything written in it. Then you will be prosperous and successful." (Joshua 1:8)

"But remember the LORD your God, for it is he who gives you the ability to produce wealth, and so confirms his covenant, which he swore to your forefathers, as it is today." (Deuteronomy 8:18)

In developing a mindset of wealth, abundance, and prosperity, remember this action checklist:

✓ Reevaluate your perspective about your possessions and resources;

✓ Cultivate and maintain an attitude of gratitude for what you do have;

✓ Condition your mind to recognize that you are successful and have wealth, abundance, and prosperity right now;

✓ Present yourself in excellence and service to others, you are a valuable gift worthy of your wages and are fully equipped;

✓ Focus on God and stand in faith, believing He will provide;

✓ Study your holy book, meditate and listen for instructions, and then take action.

HOW TO HAVE PEACE ABOUT YOUR
CHARITABLE DONATIONS AND TITHES

God's Responsibility

Many people expend a lot of negative energy speculating about what charitable organizations do with the monetary contributions that are donated. These people will often use the proven violators and abusers of the system as an excuse not to give or to give in part, like with tithing to the church. However, I suggest to you that if you keep your eyes fixed on Jesus, the author and finisher of your faith, and do what the Word says in regards to giving, you will receive your just reward and so will the receiver who misappropriates those funds.

"Therefore judge nothing before the appointed time; wait till the Lord comes. He will bring to light what is hidden in darkness and will expose the motives of men's hearts. At that time each will receive his praise from God." (1 Corinthian 4:5)

God sees and knows our heart, remember the story of Ananias and Sapphira in Acts 5:1-11. They sold a piece of property to give the money to the church; but, they kept part of the money for themselves and lied about the selling price to the apostles. The couple had actually lied to God and fell down dead because of their sin.

In John 21:22 after Peter questioned Jesus about another disciple who was following them, Jesus answered, "*If I want him to remain alive until I return, what is that to you? You must follow me.*" In other words, you do what God requires of you and don't concern yourself with anyone else's business, motives, or behavior.

Our Responsibility and Reward

"But just as you excel in everything —in faith, in speech, in knowledge, in complete earnestness and in your love for us— see that you also excel in this grace of giving." (2 Corinthians 8:7)

2 Corinthians 9:6-11 tells us that we ought to cheerfully sow generously what we have decided in our hearts because then, God will supply and increase our seed and will enlarge the harvest of our righteousness; and we will be made rich in every way so that we can be generous on every occasion.

Luke 6:38 says to *"Give, and it will be given to you. A good measure, pressed down, shaken together and running over, will be poured into your lap. For with the measure you use, it will be measured to you."*

Giving in accordance to God's kingdom system will produce an abundant return and is the best trustworthy financial increase strategy this side of heaven.

The Biblical Principle of Tithing

Many people struggle with the whole 10% tithing principle and also question if they should tithe on the gross or the net amount of their income. One preacher once posed the question, "Do you want God to bless you on your gross or the net?" That settled it for me; I'll take a gross blessing over a net blessing any day!

Tithing is not an option. In Malachi 3:6-12, God considers it robbery to not pay tithes and tells the people to turn back to Him and He would return to them when they paid their tithes and offerings.

"I the LORD do not change. So you, O descendants of Jacob, are not destroyed. Ever since the time of your forefathers you have turned away from my decrees and have not kept them. Return to me, and I will return to you," says the LORD Almighty. "But you ask, 'How are we to return?' "Will a man rob God? Yet you rob me. "But you ask, 'How do we rob you?' "In tithes and offerings. You are under a curse—the whole nation of you—because you are robbing me. Bring the whole tithe into the storehouse, that there may be food in my house. Test me in this," says the LORD Almighty, "and see if I will not throw open the floodgates of heaven and pour out so much blessing that you will not have room enough for it. I will prevent pests from devouring your crops, and the vines in your fields will not cast their fruit," says the LORD Almighty."

Pray for wisdom and discernment in your giving and when God leads you to give to any organization, cheerfully give with pure motives what He places on your heart to give, and then release the offering unto God. You have then done your part and whatever transpires from that point on is between God and the recipient or new administrator of those funds.

"So then, each of us will give an account of himself to God .... and he who gives to the poor will lack nothing, but he who closes his eyes to them receives many curses." (Romans 14:12; Proverbs 28:27).

The Tithing Principle

When you journey through the Old Testament,
you will find it amply shows
offerings for the place of worship and the priests of God
produced a mutual overflow.

In the New Testament Church example,
all believers were one in heart and mind;
all shared everything they had,
all needs were met and all were treated kind.

It's time to set the record straight and break down the facts
God's intentions about tithing is simply that:

He wants to bless your life completely and sustain the church,
He doesn't need it; He owns everything in heaven and earth.
You're just returning one tenth of what's already His;
it profits your account, when you wholeheartedly give.

When you give of your best offerings unto the Lord,
He will increase you till you won't have room to store it all.
Don't worry about how you will make do or survive,
seek God's kingdom first; He knows your need,
He will provide.

The love of money leads to temptations,
traps, and will deceive,
and cause your hands to tightly clench,
unable to give or receive.

Cautious people grow poorer,
while some free spenders grow rich;
but being generous for God
helps you become prosperous.

As a measure, give proportionately to
what God has given you,
you will then live in continual increase
and be blessed in all you do.

HOW TO HOLD ONTO GOD'S
GUARANTEED GOODNESS

Holding on to God's goodness and promises when you feel lost and your circumstances look bleak requires some intentional action as suggested below. You must stir up your hope and guard your heart because the issues of life flow out of it. Don't allow situations and circumstances to deceive you and bind you with the fear factor of (False Evidence Appearing Real).

1.   **Remember Who You Are And Whose You Are**:

    • You are a fearfully and wonderfully made;

    • You are more than a conqueror;

    • You are a creation of God with the ability to do all things through Christ who strengthens you;

    • God is the Great I AM, who does all things well, in whom nothing is impossible;

    • God loves you unconditionally;

• God has set his seal of ownership on you, and put his Spirit in your heart as a deposit, guaranteeing what is to come.

2.   **Maintain A Right Mindset**: Know and expect to experience challenges and if you haven't yet, just keep living. Trials are necessary to grow and develop you personally and spiritually. Understand that they strengthen your faith, provide your testimony; and your endurance encourages others. Don't worry, praise God, and be thankful in the midst. God is still good all the time. Meditate on supporting scriptures: James   1:2-4; 1   Peter   4:12-19; Galatians   6:9-10; Philippians 4:4-7.

3.   **Remain Committed To God**: Don't give up on God because He won't give up on you. No matter what you're facing, He is the best option going. Even if He never did another good thing for you, He is still good, yesterday, today and forever. Do like the 3 Hebrew boys in Daniel 3:17-18 when they refused to bow down to images of gold or serve other gods, even at the risk of being burned alive.

4.   **Trust God For Deliverance**: Not only will God deliver you, He will also be with you in the midst of your struggles and fiery trials, as demonstrated with the 3 Hebrews boys in Daniel 3:24-25; and stated in Psalms 34:19-22, God will deliver the righteous from all their many troubles.

"And we know that in all things God works for the good of those who love him, who have been called according to his purpose."
(Romans 8:28)

5.   **Believe God Has A Plan**: Hold out for the promise, don't faint or quit too soon. Your breakthrough is at hand. Be confident and do not entertain any thoughts to the contrary. Meditate on these supporting scriptures:

"For I know the plans I have for you," says the Lord. "They are plans

for good and not for disaster, to give you a future and a hope.
[12]In those days when you pray, I will listen. [13]If you look
for me wholeheartedly, you will find me."
(Jeremiah 29:11-13)

"Now faith is confidence in what we hope for and assurance
about what we do not see. [2]This is what the ancients
were commended for." (Hebrews 11:1-2)

6.   **Be Obedient**: God's love is unconditional, but His promises are conditionally guaranteed. Walk in a continuous state of repentance, expecting God's good to follow you.

"For the LORD God is a sun and shield; the LORD bestows favor
and honor; no good thing does he withhold from those
whose walk is blameless." (Psalm 84:11)

Deuteronomy   28:1-14 details   multiple   rewards   of following God's commands, *"[1-6]If you listen obediently to the Voice of God, your God, and heartily obey all his commandments that I command you today, God, your God, will place you on high, high above all the nations of the world. All these blessings will come down on you and spread out beyond you because you have responded to the Voice of God, your God."*

Remember, count it a joy and grow in God as you press and persevere through this life. Stand on God's everlasting word and hold on because He guarantees deliverance. God is able; and even if He does not do it in your way and time-frame, still trust, serve, and consider it already done.

Be confident that He is always present with you and your best is yet to come. He is unfolding a good and prosperous plan and if you stay the course and follow his instruction, God's blessing will chase you down and overtake you, and make you rich without sorrow.

"The Lord's blessing is our greatest wealth. All our work
adds nothing to it!" (Proverbs 10:22)

GOD'S BEAUTY FOR ASHES: HOW TO TURN THE NEGATIVE INTO A POSITIVE

In Isaiah 61:3, God promises to crown us with beauty instead of ashes. He will turn the negative situations of our lives into a positive outcome, an expected end that will mature us in the process. However, in times when the pain of the process causes blockages of unforgiveness, I offer the following ways to facilitate forward movement in purpose, forgiveness, and Love.

1. **Seek to identify your purpose**: Look to your pain to discover your life's purpose, understanding that the hell you went through or are presently in is not "just because" or just for you. You are being prepared to minister to a people.

- Turn within– Face those inner demons. It will help you heal and discover who you are here to help.

- Learn the lessons, remembering what you did to survive– How did you endure, persevere and overcome victoriously?

- Know that God comforts you in these situations so that you can comfort others in theirs.

2. Be willing to forgive: In order to see the beauty beyond the betrayal, be willing to let go and surrender the ashes to God, understanding that we are often co-contributors to some situations that manifest in our lives.

- Examine your role in the painful outcome and what led up to it; Ask God what and how you contributed?

- Release the bitterness and the hate, recognizing that you are only holding yourself hostage.

3. Increase your love vibration: Starting with self-love, look at yourself in the mirror and speak love; be gentle with your emotions and treat yourself nice; do things that you like and that make you smile on the inside.

- Do random acts of kindness on purpose– Intentionally encourage someone or bless their day in some way. Make a phone call, visit a shut-in, offer a prayer, run an errand. Ask God, who you can bless today and in what way. Start with a smile and a kind word. Follow the example of Jesus Christ and BE LOVE.

- Receive Love– Become an excellent receiver of God's favor and the loving support that others want to bless you with, whether it's a compliment, a financial blessing, or a gift of any kind. Learn to receive and express gratitude without resistance, experiencing the overflow of a full heart in appreciation of God's love.

Allow the pain you've endured to help you define your purpose and the target population who are, have, or will be experiencing the negative situations you've transformed into a positive. Facilitate your healing and operate in forgiveness by walking in love as God gives you beauty for ashes.

SPIRITUAL GROWTH AND DEVELOPMENT: THE PAIN, PURPOSE AND PROMISE

The Road To Maturity

Spiritual growth and development is a process of stages that takes a physical lifetime to complete and at times can be a painful experience on many levels. However, as long as you have breath, and an openness and willingness to learn and grow, you can and will experience spiritual transformation and progressive development that will enable you to live a fulfilling and victorious life.

Some of you may have been on this journey for many years and consider yourselves seasoned travelers, and perhaps some of you are new to the path and contemplate changing direction or finding a new path due to the struggles and hardships you encounter. Well, wherever you are and whatever you're going through in your journey, experience peace in the fact that God is aware and in control. He has a plan and purpose for your life that is to prosper you, give you hope and a future (Jeremiah 29:11). Stay the course, press ahead, and be encouraged through the following synopsis that illustrates experiences and comfort for the road to spiritual maturity.

The Purpose of Persevering

You are a unique individual, a child of God, molded and developed from within by the Holy Spirit. You encounter various experiences– many you endure, some you barely survive, most of which you overcome. All for a reason, a specific purpose of growth. God has called you to persevere, so that you may be mature and complete, not lacking anything. Therefore, consider these times pure joy (James 1:2-4).

You may feel insecure in your Christian journey, confusion about proper behavior and responses. You are a babe in Christ, a novice in the ways of His 'word'. Take heart my friend, for *"we all stumble in many ways. If anyone is never at fault in what he says, he is a perfect man, able to keep his whole body in check"* (James 3:2).

Perfection is a lifetime attainment for a Christian; something constantly and continuously strived for. At times you may feel awkward and uncomfortable because of criticisms and rebukes. But, *"do not despise the Lord's discipline and do not resent His rebuke because the Lord disciplines those He loves"* and punishes everyone He accepts as a son (Proverbs 3:11-12; Hebrews 12:5).

Remember the true reality that God does not show favoritism, but accepts men from every nation who fear Him and do what is right (Acts 10:34-35). Know that you are loved and accepted because of and in spite of the things that make you the person you are.

"Continue to work out your own salvation with fear and trembling, for it is God who works in you to will and to act according to His good purpose" (Philippians 2:12-13).

And so that you will not grow weary and lose heart, run with perseverance the race marked out for us, keeping your eyes fixed on Jesus, the author and perfecter of our faith, who for the joy set before Him endured the cross, scorning its shame, and sat down at the right hand of the throne of God (Hebrews 12:1-3).

HOW TO HAVE A GOD VIEW
OF YOUR SELF-VALUE

Embodying God's view of you will transform and increase your self-value. Understand that your value is not predicated on what you do or don't do or have or don't have, nor is your value predicated on what others think, say, and feel about you or do to you. Habitually valuing other people's needs and desires above your own, knowing that it does not serve you well, dishonors you. You are to love others as you love yourself, not better than or less than. In order to value yourself from God's view, implement the following action steps:

1. **Recognize who you are in God**: The bible says that you are:

   • Chosen, royal and special (1 Peter 2:9);

   • Fearfully and wonderfully made (Psalm 139:13-14);

   • Made in God's image and likeness (Genesis 1:27, 31);

   • Created a little lower than the angels (Psalm 8).

2. **Know your limitations**: Stop stretching yourself thin,

piling your plate unnecessarily with tasks and responsibilities because you've been asked and can do the job, or because you have worth issues and are trying to please people and prove yourself. Acknowledge your limitations, know what you cannot do; otherwise, you have created a recipe for illness and disaster.

3. **Set boundaries**: Learn to say "No." Everything doesn't need to be prayed over, some stuff you know in your spirit is not for you or you don't want to do as soon as it's presented. Stop going along to get along, trying to maintain the peace because you're uncomfortable with confrontation. Some people will dump on you just because they know you're reliable and won't say no. Your time and feelings are too valuable and time is too short to be unhappy and miserable trying to please someone else, make others happy, or spare their feelings at the expense of your own.

4. **Act like you know**: Practice self-love. Treat yourself the way you desire to be treated or the way you treat others. Be good to yourself. You already have and know everything you need within. Check in with your divine self. Go to God in prayer and meditation. Seek, ask, and listen for His response and then do what you know based on His guidance. Do it until it becomes natural. Remember, we teach people how to treat us and you need to know what love looks and feels like in order to attract it.

Know that what you think, feel, and desire are important and should be valued, honored, and expressed, regardless of what others may say or think, even if they don't care or agree. Only God's view of you is the significant standard of measure.

POSITIVE SELF-AFFIRMATION

Believe who God says you are in His word and speak blessings over your life daily. It's not about what others say or think, nor is it about what you do or don't do. God has the final say and created you wonderfully with a plan and purpose. Get into alignment with God's opinion of you and see yourself through His heart and eyes.

"What is man that You are mindful of him, and the son of [earthborn] man that You care for him? ⁵Yet You have made him but a little lower than God [or heavenly beings], and You have crowned him with glory and honor. ⁶You made him to have dominion over the works of Your hands; You have put all things under his feet." (Psalm 8:4-6)

You Are Valuable

Your feelings and thoughts are important, you see,
even if they may not seem so to me,
and even if others choose not to agree.

Stand by what you believe and value yourself,
you were created with unlimited potential and worth.
There are treasures inside you
to be found when you search.

Don't settle for less than your dreams can behold,
you can achieve great success and true riches untold.
Wait for your best as your future unfolds.

Your blessings cannot be stolen or bought;
don't be in a rush to get what the Joneses have sought.
Know that the victory is yours and
the battle has been fought.

You have access to divine help
every season, day, and hour;
Be open to grow and become your destined flower.
As heir to the kingdom, you hold the keys…
you have the power!.

YOU ARE SOMEBODY

You are somebody…
Wonderfully created by the Lord.

You are somebody…
Striving to live in one accord.

You are somebody…
Filled with unlimited potential.

You are somebody…
Young, Black, Proud, Unique and Special.

You can make a difference…
Valuing your education and history.

You can make a difference…
Demonstrating God's love and unity.

You can make a difference…
Following the guidelines of Jesus Christ.

You can make a difference…
Committing to be examples with your life.

You will succeed...
In spite of oppression and personal strife.

You will succeed...
Persevering to overcome all obstacles in life.

You will succeed...
Regardless of sex, height, weight, complexion
or society's labels.

You will succeed...
Because you are determined, resilient, and able.

> *"Being confident of this very thing, that he which hath begun a good*
> *work in you will perform it until the day of Jesus Christ."*
> (Philippians 1:6)

CHILDREN OF PURPOSE

The Inspiration Behind The Poem

I wrote "Children of Purpose" as a request to encourage children, who are caught up between parents that are caught up in the court system dealing with child support and parental rights. The inspiration came mostly from feeling the pain of children within my own family, but also from what I saw and heard during my weekly commute, on the news, and what I know to be true in other families I've known personally. It was my intention to emphasize for young people that they are not at fault for whatever situations they are born into; and that no matter how painful their experiences are, God loves them, sees them, and has a purpose for their lives.

The cycle of generational curses has children, who have not been parented, giving birth to children themselves with no parenting skills or guidance to rear them effectively. Everybody is in pain reacting to each other and the children are feeling at fault, unloved, and unhappy. I wrote this poem to encourage their spirits and affirm their souls from the word of God.

*I pray that in the reading and hearing of this poem, **HOPE** would be stirred up in the core of their being and they would connect with their Creator to rise above their circumstances and conditions, soaring in excellence toward their divine purpose. In Jesus name, amen.*

You were created and born with a purpose to live life
abundantly, loved, and free from fear.
Regardless of who your parents are,
you were planned – you are God's intentional idea!

Don't believe the lies other people have told you
or the negative criticisms and profane poison they spread.
God is clear about His love and acceptance of children.
To know the truth, check the Bible,

and believe what He said.

Before you were formed in your mother's womb,
God knew you and wrote your days in His Book of Life.
His plans are to prosper you and give you hope and a future
through the powerful BLOOD and
precious grace of Jesus Christ.

It's been said, "Man's rejection is God's protection."
God understands all the pain and struggles
you go through.
He longs to heal the emotional and physical
wounds you encounter;
and for you to know you're not at fault
and He unconditionally loves you.

The Creator sacrificed his only begotten Son
to save you.
No Thing is too hard for God-
the debt of SIN had to be paid!

God's actions free you from all earthly limitations
so that the situations in your life can and will be changed.
Always remember that His works are good and marvelous
and that you are fearfully and wonderfully made!

The battle is not yours alone.
God is available and He's on your side.
He will empower you to overcome life's challenges
and work out everything alright.

Jesus said, "Let the little children come to me, and do not hinder them, for the kingdom of heaven belongs to such as these." (Matthew 19:14)

LITTLE GIRLS LOST

Faces drenched in secret tears,
Gut wrenching pain from inner wounds;
Nubian babies birthing babies
Way too soon.

Abused parents, never nurtured,
Passed down legacies of doom.
Little girls lost with thirsting hearts,
Desperate to fill deserted rooms.

Can you hear the silent screams
Echoing through the dismal night?
Can you see the fear attacking?
In the mind, begins the fight.

Can you feel the numbness growing?
Protective walls standing upright.
Can you taste the bitter fragrance?
Little girls lost, pungent with spite.

She ponders the question of:
What can effectively be done
For little girls lost to experience victory,

Live safe, and have some fun?

The answer: Accept the Lord, Christ Jesus
As your Savior and God's Son.
He will provide your every need
And become your trusted companion.

He will restore you and transform you,
Make you radiant and new.
You will blossom in His love,
Learn to receive, and give love too.

He will prepare you and equip you
With a plan for you to do.
Little girls lost, born with a purpose
Divinely designed for a unique you.

*"Therefore if any man be in Christ, he is a new creature: old
things are passed away; behold, all things are become new."*
(2 Corinthians 5:17)

A SPIRITUAL MESSAGE FOR
STRUGGLING SINGLE MOTHERS

Several years ago, God gave me spiritual messages for two of my nieces, who were young single mothers struggling with life and seeking a sense of self. Two beautiful young women with children, yet still children themselves in many ways. I shared the following messages with each of them and now I pass on the modified versions (I replaced their names with Sweetheart and Beloved) for your personal encouragement or to pass on to someone you know who may be able to identify and be lifted in spirit toward a more productive and fulfilling life.

SWEETHEART'S MESSAGE

Sweetheart, you are a very sweet spirit with a good heart. You have always been a very loveable person. You, Sweetheart, are a beautiful princess with tremendous potential to be successful in whatever you decide to do.

Sweetheart, when you finally make up your mind that you want to live and take responsibility for your life, you will be amazed at what you can and will accomplish. With God's help, all things are possible, just ask and believe.

Sweetheart, no matter what it looks like or feels like now, this too shall pass. You, Sweetheart, have a divine purpose, a future, and a hope that God wants to and plans to fulfill in your life. You've tried it your way, now try turning control of your life over to Jesus and let Him have His way.

Sweetheart, you have survived many challenges and deep sorrow. For each day that you awaken with breath in your body, be encouraged with another chance to begin anew. There are resources and opportunities available to take you where you haven't even dreamed of going when you prepare yourself to take advantage of them.

Sweetheart, read the bible and daily devotions and practice the principles in each. Pray and ask God to help you get to know Him personally, and then ask Him to help you see yourself through His eyes and affirm what He says about who you are.

Sweetheart, when you can see the beauty of your spirit, the power of your presence, and know your ability to do all things through Christ who gives you strength; your entire world will be turned right side up. Your children will excel emotionally, spiritually, physically, and academically and they will rise up and call you blessed.

Sweetheart, receive God's plan for you and choose life, so that you and your children may live, be blessed, and increase!

BELOVED'S MESSAGE

Beloved, you are and always have been an honor student. Beloved, you can and will excel in whatever you choose to apply yourself to if you do it wholeheartedly, keep your head clear, and stay focused.

However Beloved, you won't be able to fully do that until you release the anger, pain, resentment, and hurt you have been carrying inside you far too long, creating opportunities to unleash them on whomever, especially your mother and little sister.

Beloved, you have to learn how to give it over to God and ask Him to heal you; otherwise, you will block yourself from reaching your full potential and you will also pass that poisonous spirit onto your baby. Get to know Jesus, definitely, and seek counseling if necessary.

Beloved, you can let go and heal from the past if you sincerely want to in your heart. Ask God to help you want to, and then speak forgiveness and healing with your mouth. Fake it until you make it. Say it until it is so. Release the pain of yesterday and embrace unconditional love today by forgiving and accepting your mother for who she is as she is.

Beloved, you are a beautiful creation, but the internal rage is distorting your image. Although you are the only person that you have the power to change, you can set a responsible and loving example as you mold the behavior of your children.

Beloved, did you know that the power of life and death is in the tongue? Think about it– in the beginning, God spoke this world into existence. Imagine how different you might see life and yourself if you had received positive affirmations of love, beauty, and your ability to excel. Do not speak what it is or how you feel, instead speak how and what you want it to be. Do this for yourself and others.

Beloved, if you change your thoughts, your heart will follow. Then change will show itself in your life. When you change, your world and the people around you will begin to change as well.

Beloved, you cannot change the past and tomorrow is not promised, so all you have is the gift of today to do your best. Your actions and attitudes influence and affect everyone around you. Decide each day whether that influence will be positive or negative.

Beloved, Choose Life! Be positive and let your Spiritual Light Shine the way it was intended by God for His glory.

The Nature of Influence

You have influence with everybody
whether it is positive or negative.
'How you use it' is a choice
to be made about how you'll live.

When you speak, what are you saying?
What tone do you use and what pitch is it in?
Is it encouraging to the hearer?
What sort of impression will you choose to give?

When you are writing how you feel
about issues or ideals that you believe,
how do your words influence the readers?
What type of legacy do you choose to leave?

Are your actions kind and caring,
helpful, generous and true?
Is your behavior to be modeled?
Will people aspire to be like you?

Youth and adults both have the power
to uplift others and heal their hearts;
The power to step up and be responsible
as a positive influence, each doing their part.

A positive or negative influence,
choose today which one you'll be.
Then apply it daily to each thought and action
throughout your life journey, continually.

TRUE BEAUTY

True beauty must be cultivated from the inside
to last forever and never fade.
Being Christ-like in thought, word and action
will reflect the God-image in whom you were made.

Self-love is a key component
to receive, radiate and give joy, peace and love,
to be in alignment with God's greatest commandment
and to fulfill His will as in heaven above.

Extreme self-care is also important,
it includes the mental, emotional,
spiritual and physical too.
But if your main focus is only on the outer appearance,
it will create an unhealthy imbalance within you.

Don't let fancy hairstyles, expensive jewelry
or beautiful clothes be your passion and delight.
Instead, develop a gentle and quiet spirit,
which is precious in God's sight.

"Your beauty should not come from outward adornment, such as elaborate hairstyles and the wearing of gold jewelry or fine clothes.

⁴Rather, it should be that of your inner self, the unfading beauty of a gentle and quiet spirit, which is of great worth in God's sight."
(1 Peter 3:3-4)

.MY LIVING LETTER PROCESS

As representatives of Jesus Christ, we are called to present ourselves as living sacrifices. Our lives may be the only bible or spiritual letter that others read; therefore, it behooves us to get in alignment with God's will and ways, receive His love and correction, learn the lessons, grow and press forward, brightly yielded.

The following is an expression of my living letter experience:

My life as a Living Letter
was prewritten before time began,
by my omnipotent, omniscient Creator,
the omnipresent great "I AM."

God called me to repentance,
just as I was, there was no need to prepare.
God provided me the gift of salvation
when I confessed, believed and received His Love—
unconditional and rare.

It's been a "learn-as-I-go," while trying to control, process
struggling through spiritual and natural things I've heard.

At times, frustrations mounted when my growth stagnated
and when my living fell short of God's word.

I have learned: I don't have to know the details,
figuring out how or what to do next.
God orders my steps and makes my way successful,
orchestrating my world to ensure I am blessed.

I have learned to repent and surrender daily;
it is by His power I am transformed and made new.
Under God's anointing, I walk in His favor
radiating His light in everything I do.

I've learned to be satisfied and complete in Jesus
by committing to a daily, quality, quiet time.
I experience intimate, sweet and loving fellowship
that has strengthened my spirit and developed
a confident, peace-filled mind.

I'm learning to trust Jesus and reflect His image
of self-less service throughout my life.
As a Living Letter, unfolding to God's prewritten outline,
I decided to make godly choices
that victoriously fill-in the blanks.

"Your eyes saw my unformed body. All the days ordained for me were written in your book before one of them came to be." (Psalms 139:16)

HOW JESUS SEES ME

Have you ever reflected on how Jesus sees you? What do you believe Jesus thinks and feels about you and the life you live? Based on God's word, I believe Jesus sees you and me through the eyes of incomprehensible, sacrificial and redemptive love. We are precious in God's sight. The following poem is my expression of how Jesus sees me and can see you too.

Jesus sees me as the Father's daughter,
whom He died for that I might be saved.
As a much loved, unique, and new creation,
I am fearfully and wonderfully made.

As a confessed and repented sinner,
forgiven of past, present, and future sins;
As a sacred temple for the Holy Spirit,
I am filled and self-controlled by Him, who dwells within.

Jesus sees me as one of God's chosen,
set apart for His work to fulfill.
Justified by His grace and His mercy,
I am a disciple doing God's will.

As co-heir with Him in everything,
inseparable from God's love;
More than a conqueror in all adversities,
I am victorious through Him, who intercedes above.

Jesus sees me as a patient, who needs healing;
as a woman, who endures and works through stress.
As a child, needing hugs of comfort,
I am a witness, who loves God and holds to His promises.

"But ye are a chosen generation, a royal priesthood, a holy nation, a peculiar people; that ye should show forth the praises of him who hath called you out of darkness into his marvelous light." (I Peter 2:9)

MY LOVE LETTER TO SELF

Love Is...

The most essential love relationship we can have is first with God, who is LOVE. When we develop an intimate relationship with God, we can learn what love truly is and then learn to love ourselves and others. We often seek to find love outside ourselves, but love begins within. We must learn to be the love we desire to experience.

"Love is patient, love is kind. It does not envy, it does not boast, it is not proud. [5]It does not dishonor others, it is not self-seeking, it is not easily angered, it keeps no record of wrongs. [6]Love does not delight in evil but rejoices with the truth. [7]It always protects, always trusts, always hopes, always perseveres. [8]Love never fails." (1 Corinthians 13:4-8a)

Janine Ingram, author of "Born To Be Rich" and facilitator of "The Love Journey Inc" prayer and inspiration conference call, often talks about the importance of loving yourself and encourages the writing and mailing of love letters to yourself. In reading her book, I took on the exercise and was blessed by the experience. The following letter is the result:

My Letter of Self-Love

Beloved Jo Anne,

I am that I am an amazing woman of God with an ocean size capacity to love. I pour that love out on me first that it may overflow onto all others, whom God brings into my life. I am a beacon of light and love, teaching faith and encouraging souls in every season of life. Everyone and everything I touch prospers and becomes like gold. God, my Father, desires to give me the kingdom and all I desire is mine already possessed. I am a beautiful black Queen inspiring the world at large with products, information, and services.

Jesus, my Lord and Savior, gives me the power to do all things! I walk in faith, conquering fear. I receive ever increasing financial abundance, love, joy, health, peace, prosperity, and wealth in gratitude. I forgive and am forgiven. I reap a harvest of GOOD every day in every way. I am blessed to be a blessing, to be above, to be the head, to be a wife, minister, teacher, encourager, healer, faith walker, lover, coach, author, and speaker all to the glory of God. It is so and so it is!

God is the Source of my unlimited supply and for this I am truly grateful. I believe, I receive, and share as the Spirit leads. Thank God, thank God, thank God. Hallelujah! Blessed be the name of the Lord.

Love you much,

Jo Anne Meekins

How Do I Love Thee...

In writing the letter, I turned within and saw myself through the eyes of God and allowed Spirit to write the words. When I received the letter in the mail, I smiled and was excited about reading it. As I read the letter, I didn't remember writing the words that were causing my heart and soul to smile. It was an affirming experience of spiritual intimacy.

This is my letter of love to me through Spirit. What would your love letter from you say?

MY PERSONAL COMMERCIAL

It is important for a healthy self-esteem to love yourself and be able to sell yourself to you and others. On The Love Journey Inc. conference call, we were assigned a self-love exercise to write a commercial about ourselves. In order to write your own commercial, you need to put your best qualities on paper and write about yourself in an uplifting, motivational way. Include what makes you unique and a great person to know. Daily practice your commercial out loud in front of the mirror and read it silently several times a day. Tell it and sell it!.

NOTE: *Because I'm also a poet, this was how the assignment happened to express itself through me. I never know what format my writing is going to take. I simply open myself to Spirit and ask, "What do you want me to say," and then I yield to what comes forth in the manner and format it presents itself. You can write your commercial in any style or format you're comfortable with, just include the elements stated above.*

Meet Jo Anne Meekins

Jo Anne Meekins praises and worships God passionately;
and she's God's gracious gift from above.

She is an effective, powerful prayer warrior
and a jubilant expression of God's unconditional love.

She's an exceptional encourager of others
in their faith, dreams and lives.
She is a blood-washed sinner saved by grace
through her Lord and Savior Jesus Christ.

Jo Anne Meekins possesses inner and outer beauty,
exuberantly radiant with God's love, light and joy.
She is blessed to be a blessing
to men, women, girls and boys.

Jo Anne's presence brings empathic comfort;
her gentle touch can energetically heal.
Jo Anne Meekins is one with God, the Father,
and she is Holy Spirit sealed.

Jo Anne Meekins is favored by God,
anointed for greatness and to serve.
The desires planted within her compassionate,
love-filled heart are manifesting and well deserved.

Jo Anne Meekins is an appointed inspirational writer,
who can expertly pen a poetic phrase.
She joyfully dances, uninhibited in intimate devotion,
with her body in motion and her hands raised.

Jo Anne Meekins is faith-filled by
the milk and meat of God's word;
She daily applies it to her life because
faith comes by what she has read and heard.

Jo Anne is peaceful and protected,
Jo Anne is fearfully and wonderfully made;
She is a courageous, chosen vessel,
who is Christ-Minded and sweetly saved.

Divinely Inspired 4 U,
Jo Anne stepped out in faith to purposefully live.
She is a precious child of God,
who freely and abundantly gives.

Jo Anne Meekins is more than a conqueror,
overcoming challenges every day.
She transparently shares her transformational journey,
trusting God will always make a way.

MY DESERVE-ABILITY STATEMENT

Read God's word to see and know what you deserve to experience in life as His child. My deserve-ability statement was derived from another self-love exercise from The Love Journey Inc. prayer conference call; the desires of my heart; the word of God; and a message from Rev. Creflo Dollar on "Pursuing the Promises." This deserve-ability statement is infused with substantiating scripture references for your meditation and appropriation. God is no respecter of persons, what's true and deserving for me is true and deserving for you. You are worthy and justified through Jesus Christ.

MY STATEMENT

I deserve to succeed and prosper personally and professionally; to have my plans established; and the blessings of God to chase me down and overtake me because all that I am and do is yielded to God and I am obedient to His voice.

"Keep this Book of the Law always on your lips; meditate on it day and night, so that you may be careful to do everything written in it. Then you will be prosperous and successful." (Joshua 1:8)

*"Commit to the Lord whatever you do, and He
will establish your plans."* (Proverbs 16:3)

*"And all these blessings shall come upon you and overtake you, because
you obey the voice of the Lord your God."* (Deuteronomy 28:2)

I deserve the abundant life that Jesus came for me to have
and experience– the exceedingly abundantly beyond all that I
can ask or imagine according to the power at work within me.
I deserve the incomprehensible and incomparable GOOD of
what God has prepared for me that no eye, ear or heart has
seen, heard, or conceived and that works together for me in
all things because I love God and am called according to His
purpose.

*"I have come that they may have life, and that
they may have it more abundantly."* (John 10:10)

*"Now to Him who is able to do exceedingly abundantly above all that
we ask or think, according to the power that works in us."*
(Ephesians 3:20)

*"But as it is written: "Eye has not seen, nor ear heard, nor have entered
into the heart of man the things which God has prepared for those who
love Him."* (1 Corinthians 2:9)

*"And we know that all things work together for good to those who love
God, to those who are the called according to His purpose."*
(Romans 8:28)

I deserve to be the good wife, married to a loving, gentle,
romantic, affectionate, authentic, transparent, communicative,
committed, faithful, ethical, responsible, passionate,
prosperous godly man and provider, who will love me like
Christ loves the church because it is not good for man to be
alone and he that finds a wife finds a good thing.

"The Lord God said, "It is not good for the man to be alone. I will make a helper suitable for him." (Genesis 2:18)

"He who finds a wife finds a good thing, and obtains favor from the Lord." (Proverbs 18:22)

"Husbands, love your wives, just as Christ loved the church and gave himself up for her." (Ephesians 5:25)

I deserve to live a free and empowered life, and walk in healing and wholeness by the stripes Jesus endured on my behalf and because it is my natural state of being. I deserve to have every need supplied and multiplied seed to sow for every good gift and charitable donation, according to God's riches in glory by Christ Jesus.

"So if the Son sets you free, you will be free indeed." (John 8:36)

"But He was wounded for our transgressions, He was bruised for our guilt and iniquities; the chastisement [needful to obtain] peace and well-being for us was upon Him, and with the stripes [that wounded] Him we are healed and made whole." (Isaiah 53:5)

"And my God shall supply all your need according to His riches in glory by Christ Jesus." (Philippians 4:19)

"And [God] Who provides seed for the sower and bread for eating will also provide and multiply your [resources for] sowing and increase the fruits of your righteousness [which manifests itself in active goodness, kindness, and charity]. [11]Thus you will be enriched in all things and in every way, so that you can be generous, and [your generosity as it is] administered by us will bring forth thanksgiving to God."
(2 Corinthians 9: 10-11)

I deserve the fire baptism of the Holy Spirit evidenced by speaking in tongues because I am saved, sanctified, Holy Ghost filled, been water baptized, I have Jesus on my mind and I'm running for my life. I deserve to be delivered from all of my troubles and have the good work begun in me completed to the day of Jesus Christ because the eyes of the Lord are on the righteous and He is attentive to my cry.

"The eyes of the Lord are on the righteous, and His ears are attentive to their cry .... 17 The righteous cry out, and the Lord hears them; He delivers them from all their troubles." (Psalm 34:15,17)

"Being confident of this, that He who began a good work in you will carry it on to completion until the day of Christ Jesus."
(Philippians 1:6)

I deserve for God to answer my prayers, manifest the desires of my heart, and even better because I ask in Jesus' name, meditate and delight myself in Him; and God says it, I believe it and that settles it!

"Very truly I tell you, whoever believes in me will do the works I have been doing, and they will do even greater things than these, because I am going to the Father.[13]And I will do whatever you ask in My name, so that the Father may be glorified in the Son.[14]You may ask Me for anything in my name, and I will do it." (John 14:12-14)

"Take delight in the Lord, and He will give you the desires of your heart." (Psalm 37:4)

I choose to walk in repentance, love, forgiveness and gratitude daily with great expectation for divinely new, wonderful, and miraculous happenings to transpire in my life, courtesy of my Rock, Redeemer, Refuge and Radiant Light of Love and Life because my God chose me and my acceptance makes me deserving.

"But you are a chosen race, a royal priesthood, a dedicated nation, [God's] own purchased, special people, that you may set forth the wonderful deeds and display the virtues and perfections of Him Who

called you out of darkness into His marvelous light." (1 Peter 2:9)

"For I know the plans I have for you," declares the Lord, "plans to prosper you and not to harm you, plans to give you hope and a future." (Jeremiah 29:11)

I deserve and receive all God's good, planned and prepared for me, in full faith and gratitude. I believe the promises in God's Word are true for me and I go forth living life on purpose, as the authentic, transparent, Inspired 4 U expression of love and encouragement that God created and called me to be on the planet through the use of my gifts, skills, information, products and services, in Jesus name and so it is, amen!

"Then Peter began to speak: "I now realize how true it is that God does not show favoritism [35] but accepts from every nation the one who fears him and does what is right." (Acts 10:34-35)

NOTE: This is my covenant contract with God, written, printed (on sky blue, heavy stock business paper), signed and dated on 12/12/12, framed and displayed for continual accessibility to read and speak at will.

I encourage you to create your own personalized covenant contract Deserve-ability Statement to help you walk in worthiness and manifest your dreams.

MY PLACES OF SPIRITUAL FOUNDATION
AND DEVELOPMENT

Educational facilities, religious institutions, and work environments are some common places of preparation where many of us encounter both positive and negative experiences that shape us into the people we become. These places serve as formative opportunities that can lead to self-discovery and teach us how to persevere and overcome, turning the negatives of our lives into positives.

The places of my spiritual foundation and development encompassed several diverse organizations as categorized above. As I reveal how these places prepared me for and guided me into the life I was born to live, I invite you to also identify and examine your own places of spiritual foundation and life preparation. I pray that you will achieve a clearer sense of self as you experience new or deeper revelations of your weaknesses, strengths, relationships, lessons, victories, faith, and anything else that surfaces for you to examine, heal, release, or celebrate.

"For we are His workmanship, created in Christ Jesus for good works, which God prepared beforehand that we should walk in them."
(Ephesians 2:10)

MEETING GOD AND RESTORATION

Before I knew God personally, I had a strong sense that a lot of the occurrences in my life were not happening just for me. I didn't fully understand it at the time, I just had to believe that some of my experiences must be meant to help somebody else, sometime, somewhere. Through it all, God has provided some "places of preparation" along my journey that helped me become a lot closer to Him and clearer about my experiences.

New York Institute of Technology(NYIT)

In college (between 1977 and 1981) I experienced emotional and sexual violations that caused me to cry out to the Lord, "Help me Lord! I can't live in a world where I have to watch my back all the time. I need to love and trust people. I don't know how to not be me and don't want to become like them. Protect me, teach me, and keep me Lord before I lose my mind." During my time at New York Institute of Technology (Old Westbury, NY campus), a divine relationship with a Christian brother-friend, Ouemonde Brangman, led me to my first Christian fellowship group. There, the soil of my heart was furrowed to receive the seeds of God's word.

God introduced Himself and maintained my sanity in this Place of Preparation.

First Church of God (FCOG)

In 1981, Oue also led me to my first church home, where I surrendered my life to Jesus and developed a personal relationship with Him. At First Church of God (Far Rockaway, NY), I obtained a rich spiritual foundation that taught me how to live by faith, trusting Jesus for everything-the small things as well as the big things. I learned:

- To stand up for myself;

- To face my fears and do it anyway;

- To be a leader;

- That I have gifts;

- My one vote does count;

- I can make a difference, using what I have wherever I am.

During my 14 years at FCOG, I was exposed to divine relationships that acknowledged, confirmed, and encouraged my writing gift. I became the resident poet, writing for all church occasions and for one of the Church of God State publications (The Shining Light). To develop my gift and strengthen my confidence, I completed a correspondence course in Basic Journalism and Poetry, and an Entrepreneurship Program, and I started a home-based writing business, Express Yourself Creations, that specialized in personalized poetry.

God resurrected my value in this Place of Preparation.

SPIRITUAL SECURITY AND PROFESSIONAL CREDITABILITY

St. Paul Community Baptist Church (SPCBC)

In 1995, I was led to my second church home in obedience to my former husband. During my 10 years at St. Paul Community Baptist Church (Brooklyn-ENY). I was spiritually and emotionally liberated as I healed from ministry burnout, an ill-fated marriage, and awakened 20-year old traumas that I had not dealt with previously. I experienced an immeasurable level of God's love for me in my wretchedness that sustained and held me when I was too weak to hold on. I found my voice and learned:

- To speak my truth;

- To be true to myself;

- That I am a gift;

- To facilitate my own healing and the healing of others.

I discovered my purpose, my passion, and a sweeter intimacy with God through praise in dance, song, writing, and healing-touch techniques.

In wrestling with God, I learned that retreat and stagnation are not options, only pressing forward in Him to fulfill His revealed plan and purpose for my life and to testify of His faithfulness. Moreover, I learned that God's strength is made perfect in my weakness (2 Corinthians 12:9) and that *"I can do all things through Christ who strengthens me"* (Philippians 4:13).

God sealed my salvation in this Place of Preparation.

Healthfirst, Inc.

In May 2003, God orchestrated me into my first corporate workplace and a newly created position (Policies & Procedures Writer) that paid me well for doing a job I was gifted in and enjoyed doing. I was awed by God and interviewed for the position because it sought after me (I didn't know about it or apply for it). One day, I received a message on my answering machine to call if interested. I knew God had provided the opportunity by making my resumé accessible at just the right time before the right people, so in spite of my inexperience, insecurity, and fears, I stepped out and said yes to God and the subsequent job offer.

I learned how to surrender my gifts to God and trust that His grace and unlimited creativity would be sufficient to help me grow and excel in skill, job performance, and professionalism; and that whatever God calls me to, He has already equipped me to do it.

God gave me a new professional level of confidence, experience, and creditability in this Place of Preparation.

A HIGHER CALL AND INTIMATE LEVEL

Crossroads Tabernacle. (CT)

In July 2005, the Lord physically separated me from all that was familiar and orchestrated my move to the Bronx and my third church home, Crossroads Tabernacle. I visited 2 other Bronx churches with one more on my list before coming to Crossroads on August 7, 2005 and settling there for a season of 4 years. God prepared a safe place for me in my beautiful new Bronx residence and church home.

As a member of the church, I basked in the purity of the love, praise, worship, and preached Word. I learned to make God my circumference as well as my center and I was challenged to a holier and humbler walk in Him. During my first year there as a writer in the Living Letters Spiritual Formation Group, I bonded with kindred spirits and learned how to identify the moments, work through the memories, and write my story to be shared for the edification of God's people; and for the comfort and encouragement of others in need.

**God called me to come up higher
in this Place of Preparation.**

Inner Visions Institute for Spiritual Development (IVISD)

In 2006, I applied to and began attending **the** Inner Visions Institute for Spiritual Development (Silver Springs, MD), a Spiritual Life Coaching program that I had been desiring to experience for 6 years. There, I came to understand that:

- Acknowledgement is the first step toward healing;

- Overwhelm is the indication of trying to convince yourself you can do something that you don't really believe you can do;

- The enemy was the inner me;

- Undesirable traits in another is sometimes a reflection of myself; and when their behavior triggers a negative reaction in me, it is often about an inner aspect of myself that needs to be healed.

Likewise at IVISD, I learned to:

- Attune myself- listen to and honor the language of my body;

- Identify and heal affected emotional areas in the core of my being;

- Implement a Living Vision Action Plan to press pass fear and procrastination.

I also learned that I can create or obtain the emotional, physical, mental, and spiritual elements that appear lacking in my life instead of waiting for someone else to provide them; and that my creativity is unlimited and accessible because God is my ever present co-creative Source.

God ushered me into a more intimate relationship with Him and revealed to me who I am in this Place of Preparation.

Major Discovery and Decision

In March 2007, after seeking God's direction and spending time examining and healing emotional issues that plagued me throughout my life, I experienced some deep revelations and made the choice to end my enrollment at IVISD after 9-months of study. The following narrative describes what transpired in my quiet time with God:

Sitting At His Feet

Sitting at the feet of Jesus revealed a lot
about the life I lived.
I realized that my acts of kindness evolved
out of a childhood need-
treating people the way I always desired to be treated
is the motivation behind why I give.

I desired a life of fulltime ministry since 1998,
blindly striving, and doing, and running toward that goal.
Instead of sitting at His feet, awaiting instructions
and letting my journey naturally and spiritually unfold.

Out of fear, self-doubt, and insecurity,
I would get busy trying to find my way.
Until I finally got where I thought was the answer
and found that I did not want to stay.

As I studied Spiritual Life Coaching,
learning to heal and develop myself,

internal issues came to the surface
that needed to be addressed.
Sitting at the feet of Jesus, I realized
that mentally and emotionally I was a MESS!

I was so busy taking care of others, trying to
catch and keep up with the responsibilities of my life.
I started to lose myself in the process,
crashing heart first into an emotional wall;
I discovered that the life I envisioned to experience
was not the life that I desired at all.

I was striving to live a life I thought I was supposed to live,
but found it was a self-imposed prison of my own.
Sitting at the feet of Jesus, I realized that
who I was and what I wanted … I really did not know.

I chose to end my studies and slow down the pace,
realizing that in order to move forward I needed to be fully
present in the personal and professional relationships,
and the responsibilities that I then currently faced.

Sitting at the feet of Jesus, I realized that
although I am a work in progress, I Am enough!
And even the little things I do in His name
are significant to Him and the people whose lives I touch.

Sitting at the feet of Jesus, I realized that
I was right where I was supposed to be
and what I had was sufficient for where I was.

I realized that I don't have to make things happen in my life;
I daily surrender my whole self and all my attachments,
trusting God to do the work in and through me,
as I sit at His feet.

"The Lord will perfect that which concerns me; Your mercy and loving kindness, O Lord, endure forever- forsake not the works of Your own hands." (Psalm 138:8)

PENTECOSTAL PRAISE AND PRAYER

Greater Faith Temple (GFT)

On July 5, 2009, I joined Greater Faith Temple (Bronx, NY) after having felt the tug of Spirit to move on and a few visits to various churches across the boroughs. I bubbled with excitement about the amazing things God had in store for me moving forward. Greater Faith is a Pentecostal church with a non-denominational mentality; rightly referred to as Church of the Living God and Dome of Praise!. I got to freely praise and worship to my heart's content, by the time we were done I was physically spent.

God perfected my praise and prepared me to soar on eagles wings in this Place of Preparation.

Apostolic Temple of Jesus Christ (AToJC)

In 2012, after visiting churches for a year and moving back to Queens, I joined Apostolic Temple of Jesus Christ (Springfield Gardens, NY). It has been a love affair of people, preaching, teaching, prayer, praise and worship, encouragement and support. I am walking out my faith and vision for ministry as Spirit guides through this season of surrender and obedience. I was re-baptized on Good Friday that year, and resurrected with a mind to go all the way with, for, through and in God. His will be done!

God is deepening my commitment and stretching my faith in this Place of Preparation.

SUMMARY QUESTIONS TO EXPLORE

Places of Preparation, Spiritual Foundation and Development, such as schools, churches, and jobs are formative environments that can provide self-discovering opportunities of growth and victory for those of us willing to ask, be available, allow, and receive.

My places of preparation enabled me to experience a deeper understanding and appreciation of God and myself on every level of my being. I beseech you to take time to answer the following questions for your own self development, discovery, and the edification of others you will encounter along the way who need to know what you have learned:

✓ What are some of your spiritual foundation and preparation places?

✓ What discoveries have you made in those places?

✓ What negatives encounters have you overcome or turned into positive experiences?

✓ How has your story evolved through your journey?

✓ What old issues are still present that need to be healed?

ABOUT THE AUTHOR

Christian Writer Jo Anne Meekins is the owner of Inspired 4 U Ministries, LLC and Inspired 4 U Publications. She is also a Faith-Based Speaker, Publisher, Self-Publishing Book Coach, and Author of the recently released 3-volume series "Living a Vocal, Valued and Victorious Life," which includes:

1. How To Uncover, Heal & Release Painful Life Experiences
2. How to Press Forward & Shift to a Higher Level
3. How To Know God Better & Love Yourself More

Additional biblically-based books are:

- How To Self-Publish in Excellence within 10-Days: A step-by-step guide to self-publishing via CreateSpace
- For Such A Time As This
- On Solid Ground: Inspirational Poetry For All Occasions

Her mission is to inspire her customers and clients to live life passionately, on purpose and in excellence through inspirational products, information, and services. she empowers women to speak their truth out loud, value themselves, and BE victorious over unfavorable circumstances and situations; assists writers in publishing projects in excellence; and supports speakers and coaches in creating products to enhance their services.

Jo Anne Meekins is a Native New Yorker and graduate of New York Institute of Technology with a Bachelor of Science in Community Mental Health. She also has Certificates in Poetry and Journalism from Writers Institute; and Communication Skills from NYU School of Continuing and

Professional Studies. Her work experience includes 7-years as a Policies & Procedures Writer for Healthfirst, Inc., where her responsibilities included occasional trainings and the documentation of training manuals, desk aids, and policies and procedures.

As a survivor of rape, betrayal, fear, loneliness, divorce, multiple start overs, and self-employment, Ms. Meekins creates and serves to inspire hope, strengthen faith and increase self-awareness.

Contact Jo Anne for more information, bookings or services at:

- Email:JoAnneMeekins@inspired4uministries.com
- Web: http://inspired4uministries.com